CONTENTS

Page 4   What is Equality?

Page 6   Why is Equality Impor*(text obscured)*

Page 8   What is Diversity?

Page 10   Why is Diversity Important?

Page 12   What is Racism?

Page 16   Case Study: Ruby Bridges

Page 18   Religious Discrimination

Page 22   Sexism

Page 26   Other Types of Discrimination

Page 28   Moving Past Inequality

Page 30   Think About It!

Page 31   Glossary

Page 32   Index

Words in **bold** can be found in the glossary on page 31.

WHAT IS EQUALITY?

Not every person in the world is treated equally. The way someone is treated depends on many things, such as where they live, what they believe, and how they look. In some areas of the world, people, such as women, are paid less for doing the same job as other people. In other areas, people can't practice their religion freely. Sometimes, two people who have committed the same crime will be given different prison sentences because of their **race** or the place they live. Treating people differently because of their beliefs, **gender**, race, physical ability, age, or **wealth** is called discrimination. Discrimination happens in every country around the world. It is one way that inequality exists.

A **truly equal** society is one where everyone is treated and valued the same despite differences in their race, culture, sex, age, wealth, or religion.

THE OPPOSITE OF EQUALITY IS INEQUALITY.

This man is Sikh, which means that he follows the religion of Sikhism. There are places in the world where he could face discrimination because of the religion he follows.

EQUALITY & DIVERSITY

by

Charlie Ogden

Crabtree Publishing Company
www.crabtreebooks.com
1-800-387-7650

Published in Canada
Crabtree Publishing
616 Welland Avenue
St. Catharines, ON
L2M 5V6

Published in the United States
Crabtree Publishing
PMB 59051
350 Fifth Ave, 59th Floor
New York, NY 10118

Published by Crabtree Publishing Company in 2017

First Published by Book Life in 2016
Copyright © 2017 Book Life

Author
Charlie Ogden

Editors
Grace Jones
Janine Deschenes

Design
Drue Rintoul

Proofreader
Crystal Sikkens

**Production coordinator and
prepress technician (interior)**
Margaret Amy Salter

Prepress technician (covers)
Ken Wright

Print coordinator
Katherine Berti

Printed in Hong Kong/012017/BK20161024

Photographs
Shutterstock: Sergei Bachlakov: page 9; jbor: page 11 (top); Tumar: page 11 (bottom); Skyward Kick Productions: page 12; CRSHELARE: page 13; Alessia Pierdomenico: page 14, cover (bottom); r.nagy : page 15; Jorg Hackemann: page 16 (bottom); Stuart Monk: page 17; Aleksandar Todorovic: p 18; evantravels: page 19; Zurijeta: page 21

All other images from Shutterstock and Wikimedia Commons.

Cover Images
(Top) A group of rural women band together as activists called the Gulabi Gang, to protest violence against women in India.
(Bottom) Nelson Mandela, the late president of South Africa

Library and Archives Canada Cataloguing in Publication

Ogden, Charlie, author
        Equality and diversity / Charlie Ogden.

(Our values)
Issued in print and electronic formats.
ISBN 978-0-7787-3265-5 (hardback).--
ISBN 978-0-7787-3348-5 (paperback).--
ISBN 978-1-4271-1896-7 (html)

        1. Equality--Juvenile literature. 2. Cultural pluralism--
Juvenile literature. 3. Multiculturalism--Juvenile literature. I.
Title.

HM821.O43 2016   j305   C2016-906663-0
                                       C2016-906664-9

Library of Congress Cataloging-in-Publication Data

CIP available at Library of Congress

It can be difficult to describe what equality means. However, there are three main areas where equality is usually seen as most important. They are:

Rights—Rights are things that everyone should be allowed to do if they want to. They include things like being able to **vote**, speak freely, and go to school.

Opportunities—Opportunities are the chances that people have to do certain things, such as going to college and getting a job.

Status—A person's status can refer to the way they are viewed by other people in society. Everyone in a society should be considered equal to everyone else. No person should be viewed as better or worse than another person because of their beliefs, gender, race, physical ability, age, or wealth.

Children have the right to go to school, but there are places in the world where not everyone has the same opportunities to receive an education.

IN 2014, AROUND 263 MILLION CHILDREN AND YOUTH DID NOT HAVE THE OPPORTUNITY TO ATTEND SCHOOL. AFRICA HAD THE LARGEST NUMBER OF ELEMENTARY-AGED CHILDREN OUT OF SCHOOL.

WHY IS EQUALITY IMPORTANT?

It is important for everyone to be treated equally so that people feel accepted and welcomed in their communities, and so that our shared global community is a fair and safe place to live.

Equality is the first step toward making a society where everyone has the same chance at living a happy and successful life.

It is still common for people all over the world to be treated differently because of things about them that are out of their control, such as their race or gender. People who are discriminated against for these reasons can feel separated or unwelcomed in their community and ashamed of their **identity**. Equality is about making everyone feel accepted and at home in their communities, regardless of differences between them. Everyone has the right to be treated without discrimination.

An equal society is one where everyone has the opportunity to get any job regardless of their background.

Equality helps a society to become fairer, because it means that every person is viewed and treated equally.

A fair society is, amongst other things, a society where all children are able to get a good education, where everyone can make enough money to meet their basic needs, such as food and shelter, and where any person can get any job as long as they work hard and are **qualified** for it. A fair society is one where everyone is given the same basic opportunities, meaning that everyone has the same chances to achieve success. The world is not yet a fair society and some people have lived their entire lives being treated worse than others for reasons that reflect personal beliefs and **biases**. When people face discrimination from others because of bias, they do not have an equal chance to succeed.

WHAT IS DIVERSITY?

Diversity means "a range of different things." When thinking about different people, it's important to recognize the importance of both diversity and equality. While equality is about treating everyone the same despite their differences, diversity is about recognizing and celebrating the differences between people. Think about the different cultures, backgrounds, languages, and traditions that the students at your school have. You can celebrate diversity at your school by learning about everyone's differences. When diversity is celebrated in a place such as a school, everyone feels comfortable to share their **perspectives**. When everyone is free to share their thoughts and ideas, you can create unique projects and learn about something from many different viewpoints. Diversity is a valuable thing!

Equality is about understanding when the differences between people aren't important, such as when everyone deserves the same rights. Diversity is about understanding when and where these differences are important.

Diversity is important in a lot of different ways, but it is most commonly used to talk about the differences between people's cultures. A person's culture is made up of the **customs** and ideas that they believe and practice. It can involve things such as the food they eat, the festivals they celebrate, the language they speak, and the way they act. A person's culture often comes from the community, such as the country, city, or neighborhood, that they grew up in.

DIVERSITY IS ABOUT RECOGNIZING THE IMPORTANCE OF DIFFERENT CULTURES IN A SOCIETY AND PROTECTING A PERSON'S RIGHT TO PRACTICE THEIR CULTURE.

Some **indigenous** peoples celebrate their cultures with Powwows—festivals that showcase cultural art, dance, music, food, and more. This is a Powwow celebrated by the Squamish Nation in Vancouver, British Columbia, Canada.

A person's culture is often very important to them, especially if they no longer live around a lot of other people who belong to the same culture. It can remind people of who they are, where they have come from, and the beliefs that are important to them.

WHY IS DIVERSITY IMPORTANT?

Diversity is important in large societies and in smaller communities such as businesses and schools. A school or business can celebrate diversity by recognizing and valuing the differences people have. People with different backgrounds, attitudes, and experiences often have unique skills and original ideas about how best to do things. Diverse businesses understand how useful people from different backgrounds are in coming up with new ideas, and encourage collaboration, or working together. At school, diversity allows students to learn about many ideas and perspectives. Everyone brings knowledge from their background and the culture that they grew up in, so one of the best ways to make sure that an organization is able to accomplish its goals is to celebrate diversity!

Diversity in businesses can help to make them more successful.

Having a diverse society is important because it can open people up to new things that they wouldn't have had the opportunity to experience otherwise.

When communities become more diverse and people from a range of backgrounds begin to participate in their community, aspects of all their different cultures often become part of that community. New shops might appear on the streets, restaurants serving different types of food might open, and different music might be played. All of these things can make a community a better place to live. Diversity makes life more interesting. It helps us to understand and accept people for who they are, and shows us how to celebrate all of the differences between people!

Diversity can help communities become more interesting and exciting places.

WHAT IS RACISM?

Racism is the belief that humans are divided by race, that people's abilities are determined by their race, and that some races are superior to others. It occurs when people are treated unfairly because of their race. Racism and **racial inequality** exists in every country in the world, and people from any culture or background can be racist. Racism is one of the most common ways that equality between people is **undermined**.

WHEN THERE IS RACISM IN GOVERNMENT ORGANIZATIONS SUCH AS THE POLICE OR COURT SYSTEM, IT IS KNOWN AS INSTITUTIONAL RACISM.

In a lot of countries, institutional racism is an example of widespread racial biases. Institutional racism happens when racist attitudes or racial inequalities are present in companies, governments, and public organizations such as schools or police forces.

According to the NAACP in the United States, if a black man and a white man are accused of the same crime, the black man is six times more likely to go to prison than the white man. This is an example of institutional racism in government.

Institutional racism is common all over the world.

Racism often comes from biases or stereotypes that people have about certain races. A stereotype is an oversimplified image about a person or thing that is widely believed by people. For example, the idea that Asian people are very smart is a stereotype. Stereotypes can be harmful when they lead to racism. For example, due to terrorist attacks carried out by some extremist Muslim groups, some people believe racist stereotypes that all Muslim people are violent or threatening. People often learn racial stereotypes and biases from their families, communities, and the media. Often, people who are racist do not understand another person's background and rely on biases and stereotypes to get their information. In some of these cases, people are racist without meaning to be.

IT CAN BE DIFFICULT FOR PEOPLE WHO GREW UP IN ISOLATED COMMUNITIES TO EXPERIENCE DIVERSITY. SOMETIMES, PEOPLE WHO HAVEN'T EXPERIENCED DIVERSITY CAN HOLD STEREOTYPES ABOUT OTHERS.

RACISM IN HISTORY

Some countries used to have strict laws that limited the equality between people of different races. In South Africa, a system called **apartheid** meant that black people and white people were **segregated** for decades.

South Africa

This is Nelson Mandela, the first black president of South Africa. Prior to being elected, he spent 27 years in prison for trying to promote racial equality in his country.

In 1948, a new government came into power in South Africa and introduced apartheid. It stated that people could only live, work, and go to school with people who were the same race as them. Apartheid became a system that heavily favored white people, even though the majority of South Africa's population was black. Black people were forced to live in poorer communities and could be sent to prison for going into the areas where white people lived. The system came to an end in 1994 when Nelson Mandela was elected, or voted in, as president by the people of South Africa. Mandela removed the apartheid system and made a lot of positive changes in the country. He died in December 2013 and is remembered as a hero.

Many other countries around the world also had laws that denied racial equality in their countries. Between 1500 and 1800, empires and countries took part in the slave trade, forcing African people to work as slaves for wealthy white people. Many people believed that white people were superior to others. Though slavery was abolished in the United States in 1865, racial laws in the country did not end. The Jim Crow laws were enforced from 1876 to 1965. They segregated black people from white people in some U.S. states. Black people had to go to separate schools and ride on separate buses. Usually, facilities for black people, such as schools, were not given as much money. The Civil Rights movement in the United States helped to abolish the Jim Crow laws and earn equal rights for all people. Although the Jim Crow laws were abolished many years ago, many people feel that racial inequality is still an important issue in the United States.

THE JIM CROW LAWS MADE IT ILLEGAL FOR WHITE PEOPLE AND BLACK PEOPLE TO USE THE SAME BATHROOMS AND EVEN DRINK FROM THE SAME WATER FOUNTAINS.

COLORED

CASE STUDY:
RUBY BRIDGES

In 1954, the **United States Supreme Court** decided that schools in the United States could no longer be racially segregated. It decided that segregation did not adhere to the United States **Constitution**, which states that all people must be treated equally. Schools for black children before this time were given little money and their resources were extremely limited. Now, all students could attend the same school.

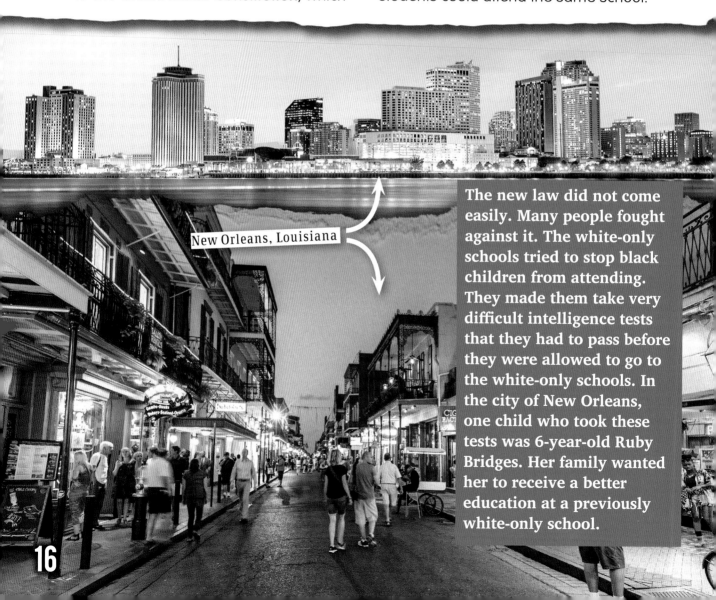

New Orleans, Louisiana

The new law did not come easily. Many people fought against it. The white-only schools tried to stop black children from attending. They made them take very difficult intelligence tests that they had to pass before they were allowed to go to the white-only schools. In the city of New Orleans, one child who took these tests was 6-year-old Ruby Bridges. Her family wanted her to receive a better education at a previously white-only school.

Ruby was the only black child to get into William Frantz Elementary School and, for the first few weeks that she was there, she was discriminated against almost every single day. On her very first day, all the white students were taken out of the school by their parents.

They didn't want their children going to school with Ruby because she was black. Ruby had to deal with people shouting abuse at her almost every day as she walked to school. At times she was even scared for her life because people threatened to poison her food.

Because of threats she received, Ruby Bridges often had to be protected by U.S. Marshals when she was leaving school.

Ruby stayed at William Frantz Elementary school until she graduated. She now runs the Ruby Bridges Foundation, an organization that helps to promote the respect and appreciation of diversity.

Ruby had to cope with a lot of racism when she was only a small girl, but she helped pave the way for a world without segregation—one that values equality and diversity.

RELIGIOUS DISCRIMINATION

Religion is often considered a key indication of "difference" between people. Religious discrimination occurs when people are treated unfairly based on the religion that they follow. People from any religion, such as Judaism, Islam, Christianity, Hinduism, or Buddhism, can be discriminated against anywhere in the world. They could be denied a job opportunity or passed over for a promotion that they are qualified for. They could be denied service at a store, or only be allowed to live in certain places. These kinds of religious discrimination are illegal in many countries, including the United States and Canada.

THE MOST RELIGIOUSLY DIVERSE COUNTRY IN THE WORLD IS SINGAPORE.

This man is a Hindu. In some places, especially those with a Muslim majority, Hindus are discriminated against.

Often, religious discrimination can happen on a personal, day-to-day basis due to a lack of understanding. Often, people discriminate against someone's religion because they do not understand the beliefs and practices of that religion. People can sometimes be unaware that a person acts the way they do because of their religious beliefs. A lack of understanding can be common in places where there is not a lot of religious diversity. People also engage in religious discrimination because of stereotypes. Stereotypes group all followers of a religion together, without recognizing their diversity or

Jewish people are often discriminated against because of stereotypes, such as the stereotype that they are stingy with their money.

individual identities. Stereotypes are often formed based on media portrayals of certain religions or the stereotypes that are held by the public, such as the harmful stereotype that all Christians do not believe in science. Learning about the beliefs, traditions, and practices of different religions can help us understand that stereotypes are not accurate. By learning about others and their beliefs, we can see the ways that we are all similar and different, and begin to celebrate the diversity of beliefs in the world.

RELIGIOUS DISCRIMINATION TODAY

Religious discrimination is illegal in many countries when it comes to how people are treated in government and in organizations, such as workplaces and schools. The United States Equal Employment Opportunity Commission states that no person can be discriminated against in the workplace because of their religion. People have the right to observe their religious holidays, wear religious clothing such as a **hijab**, and practice their beliefs in

Today, people from different religions often live and work together happily.

the workplace. They also have the right to not be harrassed because of their religion. The Canadian Human Rights Commission states that religion is a protected ground, which means that people cannot legally be discriminated against because of their religion—in any situation. Laws similar to this have been passed by many other governments, which has helped support religious diversity worldwide.

ISLAMOPHOBIA

Today, religious discrimination against Muslim people, or followers of Islam, is prevalent in Western culture. Muslim people are often stereotyped as being violent or threatening, because of the worldwide terrorist activities of extremist groups that claim to be fighting for Islam. Most Muslim people do not agree with these groups. Many Muslims have made efforts to stop extremists, and millions of Muslims have even been targeted by the groups. Yet, some people still fear that all Muslims are involved in terrorism. This discrimination is called Islamophobia. This is religious discrimination because all Muslims are being stereotyped for the actions and beliefs of a few followers. It's important that we stand up against Islamophobia in our communities, because a few extreme members of a religion do not reflect the other millions of followers.

MANY PEOPLE AROUND THE WORLD, SUCH AS THESE PROTESTORS IN LONDON, ENGLAND, CHOOSE TO SPEAK OUT AGAINST ISLAMOPHOBIA.

SAY NO TO ISLAMOPHOBIA

SEXISM

Sexism is a form of discrimination that treats someone unfairly based on whether they are male or female. It has been one of the most common forms of discrimination throughout history. Sexism is often most prevalent when it comes to women being treated unfairly, compared to men. Women often do not have the same opportunities as men. Women can also be subjected to harmful societal pressures to look and act a certain way. They are often **sexualized** from a young age in the media.

IN 2013, THE U.S. LABOR BUREAU FOUND THAT ON AVERAGE, WOMEN WERE PAID 82% OF THE MONEY MEN WERE PAID.

Today, sexism can commonly be found in the workplace. Often, women are not paid as much as men. Sometimes, they are passed over for promotions or new job opportunities because they are viewed as being less skilled than men. For example, in Canada, men are two to three times more likely to hold management positions than women. When it comes to race, the gender gap in the workplace is even more prevalent. White women earn more money, and hold more management positions than non-white women. When sexism and racism are combined, it causes even more inequality.

Sexism can sometimes come in very extreme forms. Some countries have strict laws that control what women wear, the places they are allowed to go, and the things they are allowed to do. Because of this, women in these countries often don't get equal opportunities to men, or have the same rights or status as men.

It is very common for women in Saudi Arabia to not be treated equally with men.

In Saudi Arabia, every woman must have a male **guardian**, which is usually their father or husband. Women are not allowed to travel, be involved in business, open a bank account, or have certain medical treatments without the permission of their guardian. Although women have achieved some equal rights in the country, such as the right to vote, there is still a long way to go for women to be treated equally in the country.

SEXISM IN HISTORY

For a long time, women in Canada and the United States did not have suffrage, which means that they didn't have the right to vote in elections. Women decided to speak out against this law, and fight for their right to vote. In the United States in 1869, Susan B. Anthony and Elizabeth Cady Stanton founded the National Woman Suffrage Association. The organization later became the National American Woman Suffrage Association, and was one of the driving forces toward creating and making official the Nineteenth Amendment to the American Constitution, which gave women the right to vote, on August 18, 1920. In Canada, many women, including Mary Ann Shadd and Dr. Emily Howard Stowe, fought for suffrage. Province by province, women in Canada also earned the right to vote.

Three women's suffrage activists in New York, 1912

Although achieving the right to vote was a huge accomplishment for women in Canada and the United States, not all women were given equal rights. In some areas of the United States, African-American people could not vote until 1965, as some state or local laws prevented them from exercising their right to vote. In Canada, aboriginal, or First Nations, women could not vote until 1960.

SEXISM TODAY

While there still isn't perfect equality between men and women anywhere in the world, many countries now have laws that help ensure men and women are treated equally. Sex is a protected ground in the Canadian Human Rights Commission and is also protected in the United States' Equal Employment Opportunity Commission. This means that it is illegal for workplaces or other organizations to discriminate against someone because of their sex.

Sexism is still prevalent in many places. The wage gap persists, and harmful stereotypes about women show that sexism still needs to be stopped. It's important to remember that although progress has been made, not all women are treated equally. In many countries, non-white women often have less job opportunities and are paid less than white women. To start to reduce inequality, we need to think about how racism and sexism can sometimes work together.

OTHER TYPES OF
DISCRIMINATION

Sexism and racism are not the only ways that we see inequality around the world. People can be treated with discrimination for a number of reasons. Ageism and ableism are two other common ways that inequality exists.

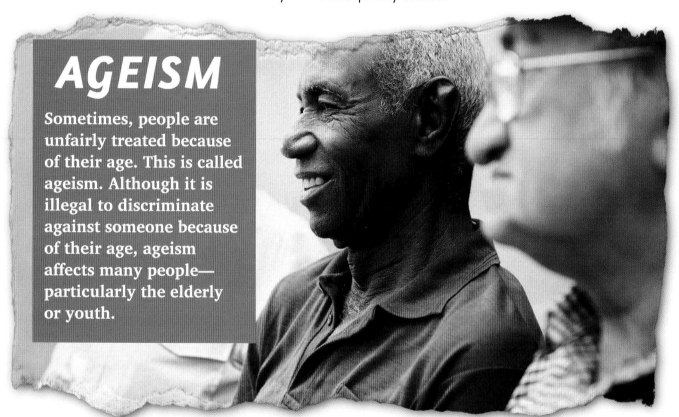

AGEISM

Sometimes, people are unfairly treated because of their age. This is called ageism. Although it is illegal to discriminate against someone because of their age, ageism affects many people— particularly the elderly or youth.

Ageism can occur in different ways. Sometimes, people hold a stereotype that people who are older do not have the same abilities as people who are young. This might stop an employer from hiring them because they don't feel they can work as hard as young people. Some people believe that older people are always unhealthy. Because of this, they could be treated unfairly in health care settings. Other stereotypes say that young people cause trouble, which means they might not be allowed in certain places. Ageism can also mean that young people may not be paid a fair wage for their work, because of their lack of experience.

ABLEISM

Not every person in the world has the same physical and mental abilities. People are diverse in their abilities, or differently abled. This means that some people live with disabilities—mental or physical conditions that affect a person's ability to complete day-to-day activities. Ableism refers to discrimination against people who are differently abled, or who have disabilities. Ableism stems from stereotypes that people who are differently abled are **inferior** to those who are able-bodied. People who have physical disabilities are sometimes inaccurately considered to not be capable of achieving certain tasks or goals, and are not treated with autonomy, or the right to make their own decisions and actions. People who have mental disabilities are sometimes stereotyped as being less intelligent or "crazy." This type of discrimination, also called mentalism, is offensive.

CLOSE TO ONE IN FIVE PEOPLE IN THE UNITED STATES HAVE A DISABILITY.

People are often discriminated against for having a physical disability, such as needing to use a wheelchair to move around. For example, communities may not have wheelchair-accessible buildings. This can cause people who are differently abled to have trouble getting around, making them feel unwelcome in their communities.

MOVING PAST INEQUALITY

Over the past 100 years, there have been many laws and changes in opinion that have helped to make communities around the world more equal and more diverse. However, there is still a lot of progress that needs to be made. Every person deserves to be treated equally, with equal opportunities and equal rights, despite their sex, race, age, or ability.

One of the best ways to help overcome stereotypes and inequality is by encouraging and celebrating diversity in our communities, businesses, and schools. By engaging with people from different cultures, countries, and religions, we can begin to learn about other people's lives, celebrate and learn from our differences, and recognize all of the ways we are similar.

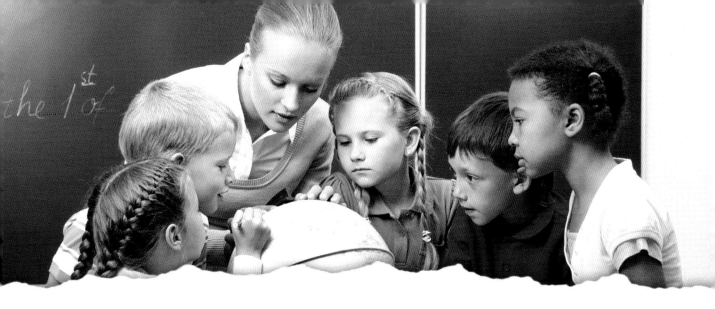

There are many ways that you can help to celebrate diversity and overcome inequality in your home, school, and community.

- Welcome everybody into your school and community.
- Show everyone respect and kindness.
- Avoid using words or actions that cause stereotypes about others to continue.
- Ask questions and do research to learn more about the different people that are present in your school and community. Get involved and learn about their cultures, religions, and backgrounds.

If we all try our best to encourage equality and celebrate diversity, we can make the world a better place for everyone.

It is up to everyone to try to make the world more diverse and equal.

THINK ABOUT IT!

It's up to us to celebrate diversity in our communities. Use these prompts to think about the ways you can make a difference.

 Think of the types of discrimination you have read about in this book. Have you seen people discriminate against others on television, the Internet, or in your community? How could you stand up against discrimination?

 How can a community show its members that it celebrates diversity?

GLOSSARY

apartheid   A legal and political system that segregates people based on race; South Africa had an apartheid system from 1948 to 1994

bias   Prejudice for or against something

constitution   A collection of rules that state how a government should work or run

customs   Traditional ways of doing things that are specific to a certain culture

empire   The land or people under control of another country

extremist   Relating to extreme, exaggerated beliefs or high levels of violence

gender   The cultural and behavioral characteristics associated with one sex

guardian   A person who is responsible for the well-being of someone

hijab   A traditional hair and neck covering worn by Muslim women

identity   A person's view of who they are

indigenous   People who have lived in, or are native to, a region for a long time

inferior   Describing someone perceived to be less important or a lower rank

media   Mediums of communication, such as television and the Internet

Muslim   A person who follows the religion of Islam

NAACP   Short for National Association for the Advancement of Colored People

perspective   A person's viewpoint based on their personal experiences

prevalent   Common, widespread, or happening often during a certain time

qualified   Having the conditions or skills needed to do something

race   Usually defined as the division of people based on similar physical characteristics, coming from common ancestry

racial inequality   Unfair or unequal treatment based on one's race

segregated   Separated or divided

sexualized   To associate a person or object with sex or sexual characteristics

society   A large group of people living together in different communities

terrorist   A person who uses violence or threats to intimidate others, often for political purposes

undermine   To lessen or weaken

United States Supreme Court   Judges who make sure the U.S. government follows the Constitution

vote   A formal expression of opinion (ie: choosing a political candidate)

wealth   The amount of money that someone has

INDEX

A
ableism   27
ageism   26
attitudes   10, 12

B
backgrounds   7, 8, 10, 12, 13, 29
Bridges, Ruby   16, 17

C
Canada   9, 18, 22, 24
Canadian Human Rights
Commission   20, 25
children   5, 7, 16, 17
communities   6, 9, 10, 11, 13, 14, 21, 27, 28, 29,
                       30
crime   4, 12
cultures   4, 8, 9, 10, 11, 12, 28, 29

D
differences   4, 6, 8, 9, 10, 11, 18, 28
disabilities   27

E
education   5, 7, 16
extremists   13, 21

G
gender   4, 5, 6, 22

I
institutional racism   12
Islamophobia   21

J
Jim Crow laws   21
jobs   4, 5, 7, 18, 22, 25

L
laws   14, 15, 20, 23, 25, 28

M
Mandela, Nelson   14

N
NAACP   12
National American Woman
Suffrage Association   24
National Woman Suffrage
Association   24

O
organizations   10, 12, 17, 20, 24, 25

P
powwow   9
prison   4, 12, 14

R
race   4, 5, 6, 12, 13, 14, 22, 28
racism   12, 12, 14, 17, 22, 25, 26
religions   4, 18, 19, 20, 21, 28, 29
rights   5, 6, 8, 9, 15, 20, 23, 24, 25, 27,
                       28

S
Saudi Arabia   23
schools   5, 8, 10, 12, 14, 15, 16, 17, 20, 28,
                       29
sexism   22, 23, 24, 25
South Africa   14
stereotypes   13, 19, 21, 25, 27, 28, 29
suffrage   24

U
United States   12, 15, 16, 18, 20, 24, 25, 27
U.S. Equal Employment
Opportunity
Commission   20, 25

V
votes   5, 14, 23, 24